Diversity in Entertainment

CATHLEEN SMALL

rosen publishing's
rosen
central®

New York

Published in 2019 by The Rosen Publishing Group, Inc.
29 East 21st Street
New York, NY 10010

First Edition

Produced for Rosen by Calcium
Editors for Calcium: Sarah Eason and Jennifer Sanderson
Designer: Simon Borrough
Picture researcher: Rachel Blount

Photo credits: Cover photo of Ellen DeGeneres: Shutterstock/S Bukley; Inside: Shutterstock: Blend Images: p. 29; Catwalker: p. 6; Delpixel: p. 28; Dfree: pp. 8, 18, 40; Everett Collection: pp. 14, 43; Everett Historical: pp. 10, 38; FashionStock.com: p. 16; Featureflash Photo Agency: pp. 1, 4, 5; Kathy Hutchins: pp. 17, 26, 39, 41, 42; Krista Kennell: p. 34; Monkey Business Images: p. 22; A.PAES: p. 27; S Bukley: pp. 21, 30; Jose Antonio Sanchez: p. 15; Antonio Scorza: p. 23; Ron Foster Sharif: p. 24; Tinseltown: pp. 3, 13, 32; Debby Wong: pp. 19, 25, 31; Steven Wright: p. 35; Wikimedia Commons: p. 37; © Glenn Francis, www.PacificProDigital.com: p. 20; Heinrich Klaffs: p. 7; Russell Lee: p. 11; Mieremet, Rob/Anefo: p. 9; Ferdinand Schmutzer restored by Adam Cuerden: p. 36; Cecil Stoughton, White House Press Office (WHPO): p. 12.

Cataloging-in-Publication Data

Names: Small, Cathleen.
Title: Diversity in entertainment / Cathleen Small.
Description: New York : Rosen Central, 2019. | Series: Diversity in action | Includes glossary and index.
Identifiers: ISBN 9781499440768 (pbk.) | ISBN 9781499440775 (library bound)
Subjects: LCSH: Performing arts—Juvenile literature. | Cultural pluralism—Juvenile literature. | Multiculturalism—Juvenile literature.
Classification: LCC PN1584.S63 2019 | DDC 790.2—dc23

Manufactured in the United States of America

Contents

Chapter 1

Diversity on the Rise

Entertainment is a wide industry. It includes television, movies, theater, and music. It could be expanded to include books, magazines, and newspapers, although the writers of those publications are often not public figures. This book will focus mostly on entertainment industries in which the stars are recognizable public figures.

Actors, actresses, and musicians are often in the public eye, so it becomes noticeable when there is a lack of diversity in their field. When the majority of Hollywood stars are white, one begins to wonder where the black, Asian, and Latinx actors are. When many of the most popular musicians in a particular genre are men, one begins to wonder where the female musicians in that genre are.

Peter Dinklage was born with achondroplasia, a common type of dwarfism. He has won many acting awards, including a Golden Globe. He is a positive example of diversity in entertainment.

CRITICAL THINKING QUESTION:
Native Americans are highly underrepresented in the entertainment field. Why do you think that might be? Can you think of any Native Americans who have had success in the entertainment fields?

Benefits of Diversity in Entertainment

Diversity offers many benefits across all industries, but there is one benefit that is unique to the entertainment industry. Children and young adults look up to celebrities as role models or idols. It can be quite isolating when they do not see stars who are "like them." For example, there is a distinct lack of disabled actors and actresses working in the entertainment field. For children with disabilities, it is a subtle message that this is a field that is not open to them. When they do see people with disabilities portrayed in entertainment, often they are portrayed in a very one-dimensional way, with all of the stereotypes attached to their disability.

When there are strong examples of disabled people in the media, it can serve as a source of inspiration for children with disabilities. For example, Micah Fowler, a young actor with cerebral palsy, plays J.J., a high school student on the television show *Speechless*. On the show, J.J. cannot speak, but he communicates using a spelling and word board. Seeing this can help inspire other nonverbal children to consider a way of communication that might not have been introduced to them.

The same holds true for other typically underrepresented groups of people, such as racial and cultural minorities, people from lower socioeconomic classes, and women. Although recent years have seen these groups have better representation in the entertainment field, it has been a slow process.

When actress Leighton Meester was born, both of her parents were in prison. Her grandparents raised her until her parents were released from prison.

USA 39

BLACK HERITAGE

HATTIE McDANIEL

In 2006, the US Postal Service issued a stamp in actress Hattie McDaniel's honor.

One of the earliest examples of discrimination in the entertainment industry is the story of actress Hattie McDaniel. The daughter of two former slaves, Hattie was the first black actress to win an Academy Award. She won for Best Supporting Actress in *Gone with the Wind* in 1940. However, to accept the award, McDaniel had to seek special permission to enter the whites-only hotel where the Academy Awards were taking place. No other black actors or actresses won an Academy Award until twenty-four years later, when Sidney Poitier won the Best Actor award for *Lilies of the Field*. In fact, over the ninety-year history of the Academy Awards, only seventeen winners have been black. The numbers are even lower for Latinx, who have only won ten statues at the Academy Awards over the past ninety years.

Diversity in Music

The music industry is more racially diverse, in part because certain genres of music have been made popular by different ethnic groups. For example, the blues was traditionally played by black musicians, but it gained great popularity in the mainstream when Elvis Presley infused his rock music with elements of the blues. Fans grew more interested in this genre of music, bringing blues musicians, such as Ray Charles and Ella Fitzgerald, to the forefront.

Ray Charles was blind from the age of seven. When he was sixteen he moved to Orlando, Florida, where he lived in poverty.

Over the decades, music styles popular with different ethnic groups gained more recognition in the musical mainstream, and minority musicians joined white performers in making up the fabric of American music.

A 2018 study by Stacy L. Smith, founder of the Annenberg Inclusion Initiative at the University of Southern California, showed that from 2012 to 2017, 42 percent of the top 1,239 performing artists were members of minority groups. Smith's study also showed that only 22.4 percent of the artists who charted on the Billboard year-end Hot 100 chart were women, and only 12.3 percent of the songwriters on the 600 top songs analyzed were women. Only 2 percent of the songs were produced by women.

Where awards are concerned, the statistics on gender diversity are equally grim. Smith's study showed that only 9.3 percent of the 899 people nominated for Grammy Awards were women.

Diversity brings much richness and benefit to the entertainment industry, as the following chapters will show. The industry and its fans will benefit when diversity is increased in the entertainment field.

CRITICAL THINKING QUESTION:

There are some very popular and highly visible women in the music industry, such as Taylor Swift, Beyoncé, and Selena Gomez. What do you think has helped these women break into an industry dominated by male artists?

Jane Fonda:

A Career that Spans Decades

The film and television industry is dominated by men, but the numbers become even more grim when actors and actresses get older. A 2016 study out of Clemson University on the roles for actors and actresses in Hollywood from 1920 to 2011 showed that there has always been inequality between men and women in Hollywood, with men taking the majority of film roles. The results also showed that women's chances to land leading roles significantly decreased as they aged. At age twenty, women got 80 percent of roles, but by the time they were forty, that number had flip-flopped, with men getting 80 percent of leading roles. In other words, women start strong in Hollywood when they are young, but they have shorter careers than men. There are, however, a few women who challenge those statistics. Jane Fonda is one of them.

Born in 1937, Fonda is a seven-time Academy Award nominee and a two-time Academy Award winner. She is also a famed political activist and ran a lucrative fitness business in the 1980s. Fonda's career took off in the 1960s, when she starred in a number of major films. She won her two Academy Awards in the 1970s and acted steadily throughout much of the 1980s.

Jane Fonda is experiencing a career renaissance since the release of her Netflix show *Grace and Frankie*.

Not Ready to Retire

Fonda retired from acting in 1991 but her retirement only lasted a little over a decade. In 2005, she returned to acting. She returned to Broadway and earned a Tony Award nomination and two Emmy Award nominations for her recurring role in an HBO drama. She revived her fitness career too, releasing five exercise DVDs from 2010 to 2012.

Grace and Frankie

In 2015, Fonda accepted a costarring role in the Netflix series *Grace and Frankie*, alongside fellow actress Lily Tomlin. *Grace and Frankie* offered Fonda and Tomlin a chance to portray two older women who refuse to be treated like old women. They are smart and independent—exactly the kind of roles many older actresses in Hollywood wish there were more of.

It is not surprising that Fonda challenges the stereotypes of older women. During the height of her career, she was as known for her political activism as she was for her acting work. She has never been one to accept anything she does not agree with, and based on her recent role choices, it does not seem as if that will change.

STEP INTO ACTIVISM

Jane Fonda's step into activism began in the 1960s, when she was a vocal opponent of the Vietnam War and a staunch supporter of the civil rights movement. Lately, Fonda has spoken up in support of the #MeToo movement, which aims to end abuse of women, particularly at the hands of men in powerful positions.

Chapter 2

Racial Diversity in Entertainment

The United States has a long and complicated history when it comes to racial equality, and that inequality has also been seen in the entertainment industry.

History of Racial Inequality in the United States

The first black men and women in the United States were slaves from Africa. Even after slavery was abolished and black people were freed, they still were not seen as equal citizens. During the Constitutional Convention of 1787, the Three-Fifths Clause of the Constitution was created. It stated that for purposes of representation in Congress, enslaved black people counted as three-fifths of a white person. The Three-Fifths Clause came to an end only after the passage of the Fourteenth and Fifteenth Amendments to the Constitution.

During the era of slavery, black people were auctioned off as if they were property.

Amendments to the Constitution

The Fourteenth Amendment, ratified in 1868, counted each person as one for purposes of representation. The Fifteenth Amendment, which was ratified in 1870, stated that no one could be denied the right to vote based on race, color, or previous status as a slave.

Even after these amendments passed, black people still lived in a segregated United States. The Jim Crow laws in the South made it clear that black people were unequal to white people. The US government believed in the idea of "separate but equal"—black people were to have the same rights as white people, but they were not to mix with them. Black children could go to school, but not with white children. Black people could eat in restaurants, but not restaurants for white people. Black people could ride the bus, but only in the back—the front was reserved for white people.

The inequality went on and on, and it did not only apply to black people. The United States also has a long history of exclusion where Asian immigrants are concerned. Chinese immigrants came to the United States to work on the railroads and to participate in the Gold Rush, but they were very much segregated. Eventually the government passed laws to limit the number of Asians who were allowed to immigrate to the United States. Native Americans were allowed to remain in the United States but were sent to designated reservations that grew smaller and smaller as the years went on. Latinx have always been common in border states such as California, Arizona, and Texas, but have historically experienced discrimination and mistreatment.

Even after slaves were emancipated, Jim Crow laws in southern states clearly separated blacks and whites.

CRITICAL THINKING QUESTION:
What barriers to racial equality do you see in existence today?

A Season of Change

The civil rights movement in the 1950s and 1960s started a season of change for all minorities in the United States. People began to recognize that race does not make people less than or greater than those around them. Although racism and inequality has not ended in the United States, more and more Americans support an equal, diverse country.

Racial Diversity in Entertainment

Given the history of racial inequality in the United States, it is not surprising that there was little racial diversity in entertainment. In the earliest US films, black characters were portrayed by white actors who wore black makeup and acted in what is known as blackface. Similarly, white actors portrayed Asian and Native American characters, too. This practice was known as whitewashing, and it continues in the entertainment industry today. In a 2018 television film, for example, Catherine Zeta-Jones played a Colombian drug lord. Zeta-Jones looks the part, but she was born and raised in Wales. In the 2016 action film *Doctor Strange*, Scottish actress Tilda Swinton portrayed a Tibetan monk. The messages sent were clear: white actors could do the job better than actors of color, and audiences would prefer to watch white actors than blacks, Asians, or Latinx.

The signing of the Civil Rights Act of 1964 started a sea change toward greater equality for minorities.

Welsh actress Catherine Zeta-Jones has been cast in Hispanic and Latinx roles.

Stereotyping

When characters of color were portrayed in film and television, they were often shown as stereotypical, one-dimensional characters. For example, black women were often portrayed as the figure of a "mammy"—a maid who helped care for the white children and did the domestic chores but was not seen as equal to the white family. Black men were often shown as lazy, foolish, and sometimes aggressive. Native Americans were often portrayed as primitive, rather than as people with full, rich lives.

A Move in the Right Direction

In recent years, there has been a much greater movement to have racially diverse entertainers in the entertainment field and show them for the multitalented people they are. Black music artists are not always Blues musicians or rap stars; they are also pop stars and classical artists. Latinx actors are not always shown playing drug lords or migrant workers and Asians are not always shown as tech geeks or martial artists.

Increasing racial diversity exposes fans to a more rich, multilayered view of people of color and the lives they lead.

CRITICAL THINKING QUESTION:

What actors and musicians can you think of today who are breaking down barriers to racial diversity in entertainment? In what ways are they accomplishing this?

Sidney Poitier:

Award–Winning Actor

Hollywood was barely past the era of blackface and still in the habit of whitewashing when a young black actor named Sidney Poitier came onto the scene. Poitier was born in the United States but grew up in the Bahamas, where his family owned a farm. He moved back to the United States as a teenager.

Poitier began his acting career as part of the North American Negro Theater. At first, he was not popular with audiences because he could not sing, but Poitier persevered. Within a few years, he had an offer to work on a film. In that film, *No Way Out* (1950), Poitier played a black doctor treating a racist white man. Poitier's acting talent did not go unnoticed, and he began to earn more roles.

In 1963, he won an Academy Award for Best Actor for his work in *Lilies of the Field*, becoming the first black actor to win that award.

Bahamian actor Sidney Poitier became the first black man to win the Best Actor Academy Award.

Faultless Men

Many of the characters Poitier played were men without any faults. This earned him some criticism: people felt he was playing unrealistic roles because everyone has faults. Poitier acknowledged the truth in this but also felt it was important to show black people in a different light from how they had been portrayed for decades before. The characters that Poitier played helped to paint a very different picture of black men than audiences had previously been exposed to.

Poitier's Accolades

Poitier worked steadily in the 1950s, 1960s, and 1970s as both an actor and a director. He has numerous awards and accolades to his name. In addition to his Best Actor Academy Award, in 2002, he was awarded the Academy Honorary Award, which is a lifetime achievement award. He was knighted by England's Queen Elizabeth II in 1974, and was given the Presidential Medal of Freedom in 2009—the highest civilian honor in the United States. In 2016, Poitier was given the British Academy of Film and Television Arts (BAFTA) Fellowship for his outstanding lifetime achievement in the film industry. He was also the Bahamian ambassador to Japan from 1997 to 2007, and from 2002 to 2007 he was the Bahamian ambassador to UNESCO.

There is no doubt that Poitier's life has seen him develop a diverse and successful career. His legacy as one of the earliest, truly successful black actors will live on for years to come.

WALK OF FAME

The twenty-six hundred stars on the Hollywood Walk of Fame are dedicated to people who have contributed to the entertainment industry. The first eight stars on the Walk were dedicated to five men and three women. However, all of the first eight people honored were white. According to Black Entertainment Television, only about 5 percent of the stars on the Walk honor black people in the entertainment industry. The numbers are even smaller for other minority groups. According to a 2011 CNN listing, only ten Asian entertainers had stars, and only seventy Hispanic entertainers did.

Gender Diversity in Entertainment

At first glance, it might seem like there is a lot of gender diversity in film and television. After all, there are many popular female actresses, including veterans such as Meryl Streep and Julia Roberts, and younger faces like Jennifer Lawrence and Emma Stone. However, a recent study of nearly nine hundred top films from 2007 to 2016 showed that there is actually a distinct lack of gender diversity in Hollywood.

The Truth about Gender Diversity

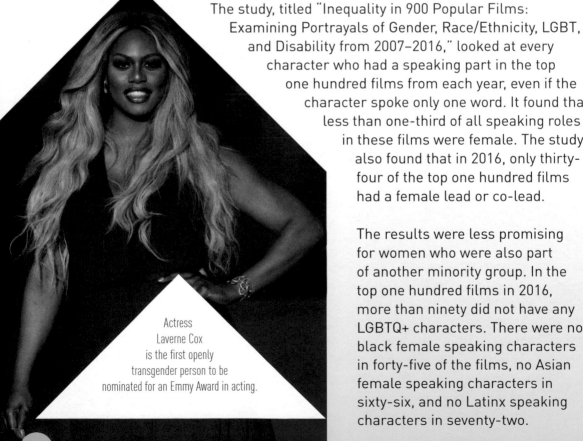

The study, titled "Inequality in 900 Popular Films: Examining Portrayals of Gender, Race/Ethnicity, LGBT, and Disability from 2007–2016," looked at every character who had a speaking part in the top one hundred films from each year, even if the character spoke only one word. It found that less than one-third of all speaking roles in these films were female. The study also found that in 2016, only thirty-four of the top one hundred films had a female lead or co-lead.

The results were less promising for women who were also part of another minority group. In the top one hundred films in 2016, more than ninety did not have any LGBTQ+ characters. There were no black female speaking characters in forty-five of the films, no Asian female speaking characters in sixty-six, and no Latinx speaking characters in seventy-two.

Actress Laverne Cox is the first openly transgender person to be nominated for an Emmy Award in acting.

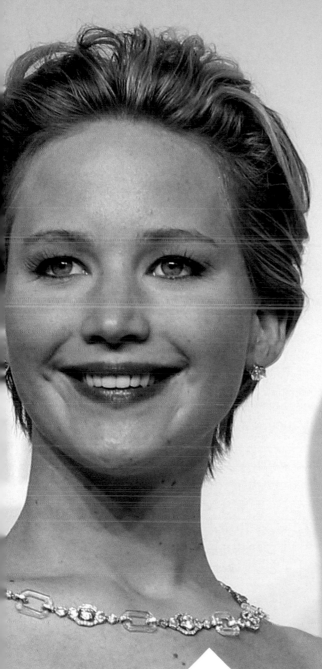

Jennifer
Lawrence
was the highest-paid
actress in the world in
2015 and 2016, and has won several
Golden Globes and one Academy Award.

Where Are the Women?

In terms of the audience for films, half is women and almost half is people of color. So why the lack of females on screen and especially the lack of female minorities? The researchers behind the report suggest that it is because the people who produce films and cast actors are mostly men, and the lack of gender diversity in the higher-up positions is reflected in the actors and actresses chosen.

According to the study, only 4.2 percent of the directors of the nine hundred films were women. Only 12.2 percent were written by female screenwriters, and only 20.7 percent were produced by women. Once again, the numbers are even lower when women are also a part of another minority group. In the nine hundred films studied, only three were directed by black women, two by Asian women, and one by a Latinx.

The report also looked at the number of LGBTQ+ characters in the top one hundred films from 2014 to 2017. In the three hundred films for those years, there were 4,544 speaking characters. Of those, only twenty were lesbian, and only sixteen were bisexual. Only one was transgender. Male LGBTQ+ actors fared better, with sixty-seven characters out of the 4,544, but the number is still low.

Gender Diversity in Music

The same team that researched movies also did a five-year study on gender diversity in the music industry. The study found that among Grammy nominees from 2012 to 2017, more than 90 percent were men. A total of 1,239 artists were studied, and the study found that men outnumbered women by a ratio of 3.5 to 1.

Much like their study on diversity in film, this study showed that the executives in the music industry are also mostly men. Only 12 percent of songwriters of the top one hundred songs for each year over the period studied were women, and only 2 percent of the producers were women. Out of 651 producers for the six hundred songs studied, only two were women of color.

Taylor Swift may be the musical equivalent of Jennifer Lawrence: a well-regarded, highly talented woman in a male-dominated industry.

The Importance of Gender Diversity in Entertainment

Gender diversity is important in entertainment because many children look to celebrities as examples of what life is really like. When they see women always playing the funny sidekick or the beautiful girlfriend, it sends a message: This is what women are. They are the funny best friends or beautiful dates and they are not powerful leaders. While there is nothing wrong with women being beautiful or funny, the problem occurs when that is the only role they appear to play. In real life, women can be a funny best friend and a powerful leader.

Women can be beautiful and intelligent. They can also be ordinary looking and have strong qualities—a portrayal that is rarely seen in television or film. Increasing gender diversity can help break these stereotypes and demonstrate that women are not just one-dimensional.

The same goes for LGBTQ+ characters. When these characters are portrayed on the screen, it is often in a stereotypical way. Gay male characters are often divas and lesbians are often tough women working in male-dominated jobs. While some LGBTQ+ people do have these characteristics, there are many LGBTQ+ people who do not fit these stereotypes. It is important that audiences see accurate portrayals of LGBTQ+ people, so that society does not continue to stereotype them based on what they see on a screen.

American Idol runner up Clay Aiken is an openly gay singer, actor, and activist.

CRITICAL THINKING QUESTION:

What portrayals of female or LGBTQ+ characters can you think of that effectively show strong, diverse, realistic characters? What makes the portrayals more realistic?

Ellen DeGeneres:

Opening Doors for the LGBTQ+ Community

In 1997, Ellen DeGeneres was sailing along on a strong career. She was starring in a sitcom called *Ellen* after having made a name for herself as a comedienne with appearances on *The Tonight Show* and in many films. Then, she made the decision to come out as a lesbian on *The Oprah Winfrey Show.*

Don't Ask, Don't Tell!

The fact that DeGeneres was a lesbian was not necessarily a surprise to a lot of people—there had been rumors for years. But at that time, LGBTQ+ issues were not addressed in mainstream television and film very much. It was a sort of "don't ask, don't tell" environment. After DeGeneres came out as a lesbian, her character on *Ellen* did the same. DeGeneres became the first openly lesbian actress to play an openly lesbian character on television.

DeGeneres secretly lived as a lesbian for years before officially coming out to the world on Oprah's talk show.

Although the episode of *Ellen* in which DeGeneres' character came out was critically acclaimed, earned an Emmy Award, and had wide support in Hollywood, it generated a lot of backlash, too. The production studio received angry letters, including one signed by at least thirty people, two of whom were influential religious leaders, stating that the show was blatantly trying to promote homosexuality. The cast and crew were subject to threats of violence and death. Oprah Winfrey, who appeared in the episode and to whom DeGeneres came out, received hate mail. A year later, the show was canceled, and some wondered if DeGeneres' career would survive.

A Flourishing Career

As it turned out, her career not only survived, it flourished. After a few lean years in which she did not find much work, DeGeneres played the voice of Dory in Pixar's *Finding Nemo* (2003). That same year, she launched *The Ellen DeGeneres Show*, her popular and long-running daytime talk show.

The Ellen Degeneres Show has achieved critical success. In its first season, it was nominated for eleven Daytime Emmy Awards and won four of them. In 2017, the show made history by winning the Best Entertainment Talk Show Emmy for the tenth time, breaking the record previously set by *The Oprah Winfrey Show*. By 2017 the show had won a jaw-dropping thirty Emmys. Clearly, viewers and critics do not have an issue with DeGeneres' sexuality. The show does not focus on LGBTQ+ issues, but being true to herself and her viewers, DeGeneres does not shy away from these topics.

In 2016, President Barack Obama bestowed the Presidential Medal of Freedom on DeGeneres. DeGeneres took a bold step and opened doors for the LGBTQ+ community—and it paid off.

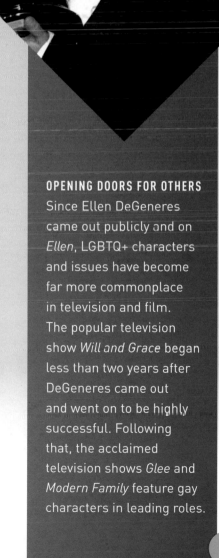

OPENING DOORS FOR OTHERS
Since Ellen DeGeneres came out publicly and on *Ellen*, LGBTQ+ characters and issues have become far more commonplace in television and film. The popular television show *Will and Grace* began less than two years after DeGeneres came out and went on to be highly successful. Following that, the acclaimed television shows *Glee* and *Modern Family* feature gay characters in leading roles.

Economic and Social Diversity in Entertainment

There are two main paths to success in the entertainment world. Some people are just born with raw talent that naturally develops over time as they work at their craft, with no formal, high-level training needed. Other people are born with talent but also have the financial means to attend prestigious schools to help them hone their craft.

Some people cross over both of the above paths. If a person has enough raw talent but not the financial means to attend a prestigious school, sometimes they are offered a scholarship. But in general, the wealthy are able to attend well-regarded programs and less privileged people must work odd jobs just to cobble together enough money to live while they try to get their big break.

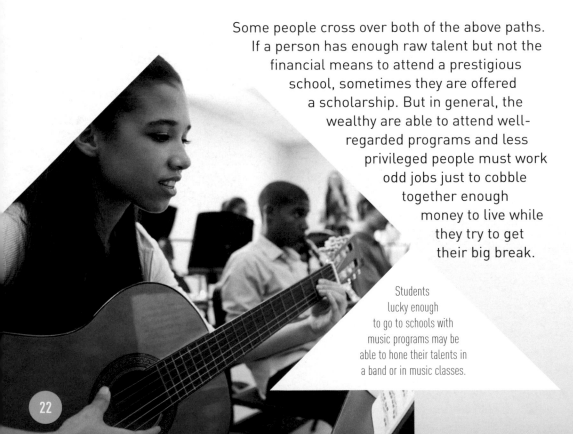

Students lucky enough to go to schools with music programs may be able to hone their talents in a band or in music classes.

A Formal Education

The entertainment industry benefits from including people from different backgrounds. Aspiring actors or musicians who attend performing arts schools can learn from masters of the craft. Well-known programs, at places like Juilliard and Tisch, attract the best of the best in terms of professors and students. Those who attend can work alongside masters and refine their own talent by learning from them.

Attendees of these programs have the benefit of having an impressive degree behind them when they go for auditions. Someone auditioning for the New York Philharmonic, for example, will be well-placed if they have a background in studying music at the Eastman School of Music. And a graduate from the Yale School of Drama has the distinction of having been educated at the institution that produced Oscar winners Meryl Streep, Jodie Foster, and Lupita Nyong'o.

The School of Hard Knocks

Actors and musicians who are able to attend these schools bring a lot to the entertainment field, but others can as well. Some actors and musicians who never attended advanced programs have gone on to become legends in their field.

CRITICAL THINKING QUESTION:
What other benefits do you think actors and musicians bring to the field when they grow up wealthy or at least comfortable? What unique experiences do they bring to their craft?

Alicia Keys was raised in Hell's Kitchen, a traditionally gritty area of New York City. However, her mother made sure she attended music and dance classes as she grew up.

Talk show host, actress, producer, and media mogul Oprah Winfrey was raised in extreme poverty. She was born to an unwed teenage mother, who left Winfrey with her grandmother for the first six years of her life. After age six, Winfrey bounced between living with her mother in inner-city Milwaukee, living with her father in Nashville, and running away from home.

Winfrey's skill at public speaking earned her a scholarship to Tennessee State University. She studied communication there, while working part-time at a news station. She worked her way up through numerous positions in news reporting and ultimately found fame when she began hosting *The Oprah Winfrey Show* in 1986. Viewers found Oprah to be genuine, relatable, and empathetic, and guests on her show tended to share things they might not have shared with other hosts. Oprah interviewed many wealthy, big-name stars, and it was not long before Oprah herself was very wealthy. However, she never forgot her difficult upbringing, and she would often draw on it to make guests and viewers understand that she knew what it was like to experience hardship.

David Letterman, another popular television talk-show host, interviewed Oprah at Ball State University in Indiana in 2012.

Oprah moved into acting and directing at around the time her talk show began. Several of the movies she acted in or produced featured black women living in unfortunate situations. She was nominated for an Academy Award for her performance in *The Color Purple* (1985), a movie based on a book about the problems black women faced in the United States during the early twentieth century. In *Beloved* (1998) she starred as a slave. Oprah also produced a made-for-television version of the novel *Their Eyes Were Watching God*, which details the life of a black woman growing up in the rural Jim Crow South.

Phenomenally successful rapper and businessman Jay-Z was raised by a single mother in a housing project in Brooklyn, New York City, after his father abandoned the family.

The Benefits of Economic Diversity in Film and Television

Stars like Oprah keep audiences aware that poverty exists and is a very real problem in the United States. They bring a much-needed realism to the entertainment field. They are also inspirations to children growing up in poverty who dream of someday making a name for themselves. So are musicians like Justin Bieber, who grew up poor and living in housing projects, the son of a young single mother. Stars who came from little, but worked incredibly hard to make it big, show young audiences that it is possible to achieve their dreams.

CRITICAL THINKING QUESTION:
Can you think of ways the film, television, and music industries could work to provide opportunities to aspiring actors and musicians who do not have the means to attend classes or go to auditions?

25

Justin Bieber:

Musical Superstar

Justin Bieber is a young man, but he is already worth more than $200 million. Since he came onto the music scene in 2009, he has released several albums, including his triple-platinum full-length debut album, *My World 2.0.* He is one of the best-selling music artists in the world, with sales of more than 140 million units. He is also an extremely popular social media figure, becoming only the second person to reach 100 million Twitter followers and the first artist to pass 10 billion video views on Vevo. Bieber has won numerous awards, including two American Music Awards and a Grammy. *Forbes* magazine has repeatedly named him one of the ten most powerful celebrities in the world.

From Humble Beginnings

This is a far cry from where Bieber started. He was born in 1994 in Ontario, Canada, to a single mother. Pattie Mallette was only seventeen when she became pregnant with Bieber, and she spent part of her pregnancy living in a Salvation Army home for troubled pregnant teens. After Bieber was born, Mallette raised him with the help of her mother and stepfather. She worked at low-paying jobs while living with Bieber in low-income housing.

INSPIRATION

Like most musicians, Bieber has songs that have inspired him throughout his career. From Michael Jackson's "Man in the Mirror," R. Kelly's "I Believe I Can Fly," and Boyz II Men's "Dear God" to two of his own songs, "Never Say Never" and "Down to Earth," Bieber has been inspired by others and in turn, he will inspire many other young musicians.

One might expect, under such circumstances, Bieber would have had a difficult childhood. But he was a strong student who graduated with a 4.0 GPA. All the while he taught himself piano, guitar, and trumpet, and he took drum lessons. Bieber used his musical talent to busk outside the Avon Theatre in Stratford, where he grew up, earning $150 to $200 per day during the high season.

YouTube Sensation

Bieber's mother soon realized that he was very talented and posted videos of him singing on YouTube. She had high hopes that he would become a Christian singer, but instead, one of Bieber's YouTube performances was discovered by record-label owner Scooter Braun. Braun tracked down Bieber and spoke to Mallette about letting the thirteen-year-old Bieber come to Atlanta, Georgia, to record some demos for Braun and R&B star Usher.

Despite her concerns, Mallette agreed to let Bieber go, and the rest is history. Bieber was signed to the Raymond Braun Media Group, run by Braun and Usher, and he and and his mother moved to Atlanta permanently.

While Bieber has had some ups and downs in his personal life as he has adjusted to becoming incredibly rich and famous at a young age, he has remained strong in his faith and close to his mother and stepfather.

Justin Bieber regularly performs in front of sell-out crowds. Here he is performing in Rio de Janeiro, Brazil, in 2011.

Cultural Diversity in Entertainment

The entertainment industry, particularly films and television, often portray scenes of white US culture. Sometimes, even when a studio tries to portray another culture, the depiction is not very accurate.

Culture and Race

Culture is not the same as race, although sometimes the two are linked. The word culture is used to describe the customs, social norms, achievements, and arts of people from a particular group or nation. So, for example, a black culture exists among many black people in the United States, but not necessarily all black people. Black people who were born and raised in Africa and then came to the United States may have a different culture from those born in the United States and whose families have been there for generations.

The inscription at the base of the Statue of Liberty welcomes people to the United States: "Give me your tired, your poor, your huddled masses yearning to breathe free..."

The Melting Pot

The United States has always been a melting pot of cultures. In its earliest days, Native Americans populated the land that now makes up the United States.

CRITICAL THINKING QUESTION:

What misrepresentations of culture have you seen in television or movies?

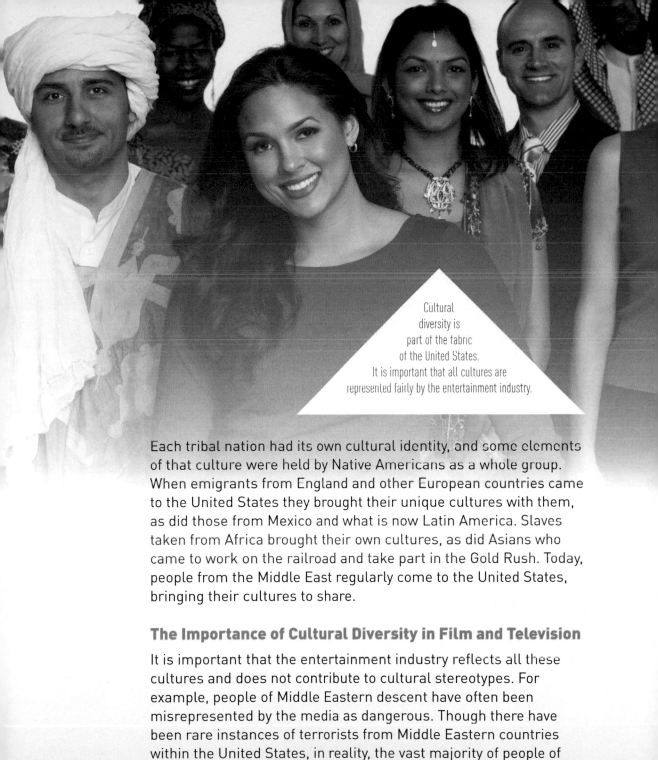

Cultural diversity is part of the fabric of the United States. It is important that all cultures are represented fairly by the entertainment industry.

Each tribal nation had its own cultural identity, and some elements of that culture were held by Native Americans as a whole group. When emigrants from England and other European countries came to the United States they brought their unique cultures with them, as did those from Mexico and what is now Latin America. Slaves taken from Africa brought their own cultures, as did Asians who came to work on the railroad and take part in the Gold Rush. Today, people from the Middle East regularly come to the United States, bringing their cultures to share.

The Importance of Cultural Diversity in Film and Television

It is important that the entertainment industry reflects all these cultures and does not contribute to cultural stereotypes. For example, people of Middle Eastern descent have often been misrepresented by the media as dangerous. Though there have been rare instances of terrorists from Middle Eastern countries within the United States, in reality, the vast majority of people of Middle Eastern descent living in the United States are respectable, upstanding citizens. However, television shows like *Homeland* reinforce the idea that people from the Middle East are potential terrorist threats to the United States.

Johnny Depp raised concern when he played Tonto in *The Lone Ranger*, a role many felt should have gone to a Native American actor.

Similarly, Native American culture has long been misrepresented in the US entertainment industry. Native Americans are sometimes shown as violent and primitive. The rich, diverse cultures of Native people are lumped together. This is not an accurate portrayal of Native Americans.

Whitewashing Film and Television

An additional problem is the use of white actors to portray characters from another culture. For example, Johnny Depp, who is not Native American, played the Native American character Tonto in a 2013 film version of *The Lone Ranger*. In the film *A Beautiful Mind* (2001) mathematician John Forbes Nash's El Salvadorian wife, Alicia, was portrayed by actress Jennifer Connelly, who is not from Central America.

When the entertainment industry embraces cultural diversity in film and television, it helps break down stereotypes. Sometimes it is done very well. For example, *Smoke Signals* is a 1998 film written by Native American Sherman Alexie. One of Alexie's goals in making the film was to accurately represent Native American culture and to put the story in the hands of Native Americans, since it centers on them. The film was created by an all Native American crew.

Another recent film that took pains to accurately represent a particular culture is 2013's *12 Years a Slave*. The screenplay was adapted by black screenwriter John Ridley IV from an 1853 slave memoir. The film's director, Steve McQueen, won the Academy Award for Best Picture for the movie, making him the first black filmmaker to win the honor.

The Importance of Cultural Diversity in the Music Industry

Musicians have long been inspired by the musical styles of other cultures. While the music industry in the United States is largely dominated by white people, there is a bit more diversity because some of the most popular genres of music are influenced by music from other cultures. For example, rap and hip-hop are popular genres of music with many Americans, and both are emblematic of black culture. Jazz was partly inspired by the music people from Africa brought with them to the United States. The famous power chord, which has been used in rock music for decades, comes from a song by Link Wray, a Native American musician from North Carolina.

It is hard to imagine American music without the rich influences of many diverse cultures.

Acclaimed actress Lupita Nyong'o and director Steve McQueen (*third and fourth from left, respectively*) were among the cast and crew to attend the *12-Years a Slave* premiere in 2013.

Lupita Nyong'o:

Kenyan–Mexican Award Winner

Academy Award winner Lupita Nyong'o brings a diverse mix of cultures to her work. She was born in Mexico City, Mexico, in 1983 but was raised in Africa, in Kenya. Although both of her parents are Kenyan, her father was a visiting professor at a college in Mexico City. The family lived in Mexico City for just four years, moving back to Kenya when Lupita was not even a year old. Nyong'o has dual citizenship and she considers herself Kenyan-Mexican.

Nairobi to Yale

Nyong'o grew up in a middle-class suburb in Kenya's capital, Nairobi. When she was sixteen, her parents felt she should learn Spanish, so they sent her back to Mexico for seven months, allowing her to revisit the Mexican part of her culture. She graduated from school in Kenya and then moved to the United States for college. She studied film and theater. Black actresses Whoopi Goldberg and Oprah Winfrey were some of her inspirations for pursuing an acting career. As an adult, she has moved between the United States and Kenya, working in the entertainment industry in both countries. She has acted, written, directed, and produced movies. Nyong'o completed a master's degree in acting from the Yale School of Drama.

Nyong'o lives primarily in the United States, though she often returns to Kenya. She speaks fluent Spanish, English, Luo, and Swahili (the latter two being African languages).

A Masterful Performance

After earning her master's, Nyong'o was cast in the 2013 film *12 Years a Slave*. She played a slave at a Louisiana plantation, and her performance won critical acclaim. She was nominated for numerous Golden Globe, BAFTA, and Screen Actors Guild (SAG) awards, and won Best Supporting Actress SAG and Academy Awards. Winning the Academy Award made Nyong'o the first Kenyan actress to win the Academy Award, as well as the first Mexican actress to win the award. It was a fitting accolade that paid tribute to both sides of her cultural heritage. Nyong'o has also acted on stage. In 2015, she was nominated for a Tony Award for her role in the play *Eclipsed* and won an Obie Award and a Theatre World Award for the same role.

SOLOMON NORTHUP

The film *12 Years a Slave* is an adaptation of an 1853 memoir by Solomon Northup. Northup was born free in New York. His father was a freed slave, and his mother was a free woman. Northup was a professional violinist. In 1841, he took a job as a traveling musician and went to Washington, DC, where slavery was legal at the time. While there, he was kidnapped and sold as a slave. He was held as a slave for twelve years, until word was sent to Northup's family to let them know what had happened. The slave trader who sold Northup was acquitted of the crime because Northup was not allowed to testify at the trial—black people were not allowed to testify against white people in Washington, DC, at that time. In the film Nyong'o plays Northup's friend and fellow slave, Patsey.

Diverse Abilities in Entertainment

For a very long time, diverse abilities and disabilities were negatively perceived in the United States. People who looked or behaved differently from the norm were discriminated against and hidden away. Slowly, new efforts are being made to shift this attitude and celebrate uniqueness.

Hiding Disability

For centuries, disability held great stigma in the United States. It was seen as something to be hidden away. It was common for famous families that had a child with a disability to hide the child in an institution—and to never visit that child. This was not only the case with famous or wealthy families, either. Up until as late as the 1980s, it was not uncommon for families that had a baby with a disability to be encouraged to place their child in an institution. Many of these children grew into adulthood without ever leaving the institution.

Even if families chose to take their disabled child

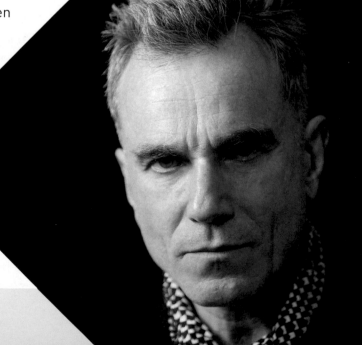

Daniel Day-Lewis famously played a writer and artist with cerebal palsy in *My Left Foot*.

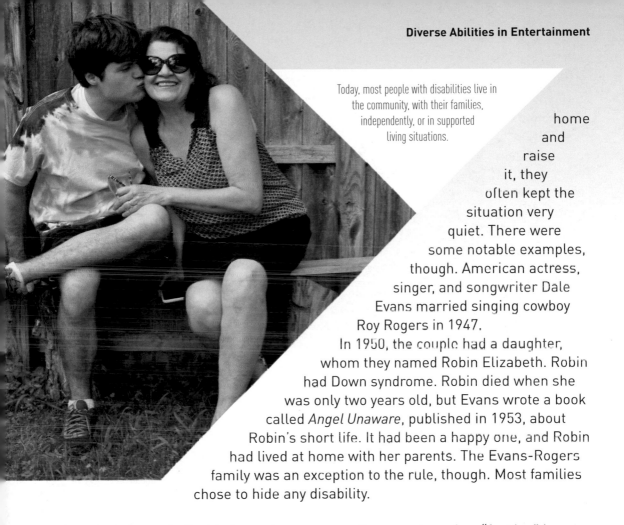

Today, most people with disabilities live in the community, with their families, independently, or in supported living situations.

home and raise it, they often kept the situation very quiet. There were some notable examples, though. American actress, singer, and songwriter Dale Evans married singing cowboy Roy Rogers in 1947. In 1950, the couple had a daughter, whom they named Robin Elizabeth. Robin had Down syndrome. Robin died when she was only two years old, but Evans wrote a book called *Angel Unaware*, published in 1953, about Robin's short life. It had been a happy one, and Robin had lived at home with her parents. The Evans-Rogers family was an exception to the rule, though. Most families chose to hide any disability.

In entertainment, disabled people were sometimes portrayed as "freaks," in sideshows at circuses, carnivals, or fairs. This inhumane practice continued in the United States up until the 1970s. The "freaks" used in these events were people born with disabilities (either physical or mental) and people who had been in devastating accidents that had left them with disabilities.

In Hollywood, when exploiting disability was recognized as cruel and inhumane, disability was simply ignored. And when it was addressed, it was usually by an able-bodied actor. For example, actor Daniel Day-Lewis won an award for his portrayal of a writer and artist with cerebral palsy in the movie *My Left Foot*. There are many people with cerebral palsy, and undoubtedly there were some who could have taken the role. However, the entertainment media has long been uncomfortable with disability, and while movies about it are sometimes well received, as in the case of *My Left Foot*, the media, the public, and filmmakers are more comfortable seeing an abled actor accept an award for the role than a person with a disability. At least, that was long the case—in recent years, there has been more of a movement toward using disabled actors for disabled roles.

Invisible Disabilities

Some people have obvious physical disabilities, while others have less-visible disabilities, such as autism. Autism is very common now, especially among boys, but it is not a new diagnosis.

Physicist Albert Einstein was brilliant in mathematics but failed other subjects. Many people think that Einstein was likely on the autism spectrum. While this cannot be proved, many factors suggest it is possible, including the fact that he excelled in certain subjects and did very poorly in others. Children on the autism spectrum often have asynchronous development, leading them to do very well in certain areas and struggle in others.

Some people with autism experience significant difficulties in speaking and performing basic self-care tasks. In Einstein's era those people were usually institutionalized because they were thought to be intellectually disabled. However, some like Einstein, who could speak and communicate and care for themselves, were often just considered "a little odd." If they did have genius potential like Einstein, then they were celebrated. Just as Einstein was a genius in his field, several people on the autism spectrum have excelled as gifted actors. Dan Aykroyd, an actor and comedian popular in the 1980s, has Asperger's syndrome, a type of autism. So does Daryl Hannah, an actress in many films of the 1980s and 1990s.

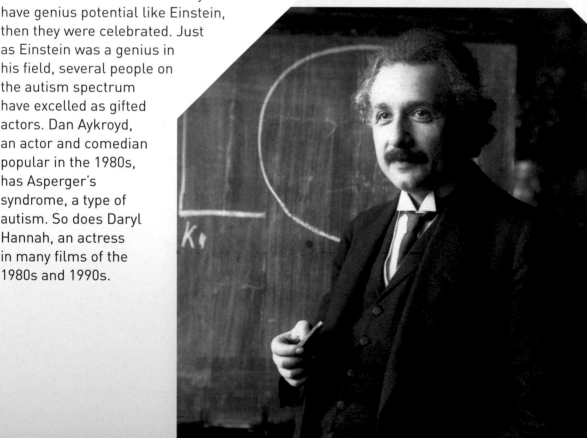

Whether or not Einstein was autistic will never be known, but certainly he had numerous traits that would suggest he may have been.

Representations of Disability

Much like the general public tried to hide disability, so did the entertainment industry. Individuals with disabilities were usually portrayed in films only if they were in some way exceptional. One such example is Helen Keller. *The Miracle Worker* was a 1962 film that told the story of Helen Keller, who was blind and deaf, and her teacher, Annie Sullivan. Helen Keller eventually became an inspiration to many people when she learned how to communicate, and so she was the perfect subject for a Hollywood movie. If she had never learned to communicate, though, it is pretty certain there never would have been a movie made about her.

People find Helen Keller's ability to communicate an inspiration. However, much of the rest of her life is glossed over, including her political activism.

The other way in which people with disabilities were portrayed in entertainment is as some sort of monster or frightening being. For example, Boo Radley, a character in *To Kill a Mockingbird* (a 1960 novel and 1962 movie), has an unnamed disability, which appears to be some sort of intellectual disability. He is described in the book and portrayed in the movie as "half man, half monster, all terror." In reality, he is a man who is disabled by his fear of leaving his house and who potentially also has some other type of disability.

Current Representations of Diverse Abilities in Entertainment

Disabilities and different abilities are slowly but surely losing their stigma in the general public and in television and movies. For example, there is a large and growing movement to recognize autism as neurodiversity rather than as a disability. The idea of neurodiversity suggests that there are many different ways of thinking, and no one type is better than the other.

Autism has gained some interest in Hollywood, with television shows and movies sometimes featuring or even starring characters who are autistic. The 2016 feature film *The Accountant* starred Ben Affleck as an autistic accountant. The television show *The Good Doctor* began in 2017 and stars Freddie Highmore as an autistic doctor.

Atypical is a show about a character (played by Keir Gilchrist) with autism that also first aired in 2017.

CRITICAL THINKING QUESTION:
Some people have suggested that famous composer Wolfgang Amadeus Mozart was on the autism spectrum. Can you think of ways in which neurodiversity might be a benefit for someone in the music field?

We will never know if the brilliant composer Wolfgang Amadeus Mozart was autistic.

While it is great to see different abilities portrayed in entertainment and certainly this does make the general public more aware of things like autism, there is one big problem with all three of these shows and films: None of the actors portraying autistic characters have autism themselves. This is a very controversial issue in the autism community. Many people feel that a person who is not autistic cannot truly accurately portray a person with autism.

To truly embrace diverse abilities, the film and television industries should hire people with disabilities and diverse abilities for applicable movies and shows. For example, the 2017 movie *Wonder* is about a boy with facial disfigurement as a result of Treacher Collins syndrome, and disability advocates wondered why the producers of the movie did not hire an actor with the syndrome to play the lead role. Instead, they applied stage makeup to actor Jacob Tremblay, who does not have a true perspective on what it is like to live with a facial disfigurement. A report by the Ruderman Foundation showed in 2016 that 95 percent of all television characters with disabilities are not played by actors with disabilities.

Nathaniel Newman, lower right, has Treacher Collins syndrome, which has been brought to the public's attention in the book and movie *Wonder*.

Micah Fowler and Speechless:

Breaking the Stigma

While disability is often ignored or portrayed poorly in the media, some shows do get it right. *Speechless* is a sitcom that first aired in 2016, and its creators have gained much respect for hiring an actor with cerebral palsy, Micah Fowler, to portray the main character J.J., who also has cerebral palsy. The creator, Scott Silveri, has made it a point to hire other people with disabilities to work on the show.

While Micah Fowler, like his character J.J., has cerebral palsy, unlike J.J., Micah is able to speak.

When he was first writing the script, Silveri planned to have J.J. use an Augmentative and Alternative Communication (AAC) device to communicate, just like his own nonverbal brother with cerebral palsy uses. But then he met a woman with cerebral palsy who had invented a letter and word board that she could point to letters or words on with a laser attached to her hat. He loved the idea, worked it into the show, and hired the woman, Eva Sweeney, to be a consultant on the show.